D1500509

ENCHANTING
CAMBODIA

MICK SHIPPEN

JOHN BEAUFOY PUBLISHING

Contents

Left: The Royal Palace complex in Phnom Penh includes the Khemarin Palace, the Throne Hall and the Silver Pagoda.

Top: The huge stone faces of the Bayon in Angkor are some of Asia's most iconic imagery.

Above right: Collecting alms is a daily ritual for Buddhist monks in Cambodia.

Opposite: Most homes and offices have a spirit house at which daily offerings are made.

Title page: The iconic outline of the Royal Palace in Phnom Penh.

Chapter 1: A Destination of Discovery

Acountry of astonishing natural beauty and home to the incredible temples of Angkor, Cambodia is one of Southeast Asia's most fascinating destinations. The fact that the country is now firmly on the itinerary of many cultural travellers, however, is nothing short of remarkable.

Above: The huge stone faces of the Bayon in Angkor are some of Asia's most iconic imagery.

Above: The heat of chillies and the sourness of limes are common features of Khmer cuisine.

Few nations have expressed mankind's creativity so beautifully through art and architecture but also plunged so far into the depths of cruelty and inhumanity as Cambodia. Over the past two millennia, a nation powerful in battle and gifted in the arts asserted its regional dominance, crowning its achievements with the wondrous Angkor, an expansive 400-km^2 (155-sq mile) site that encompassed the capitals of the Khmer Empire from the 9th to the 15th centuries. Cambodia's recent history, however, couldn't be further removed from its former glories. In the 1970s, the country's name became known for the brutal reign of the Khmer Rouge and its haunting legacy of genocide. Remarkable then that today Cambodia is a youthful and optimistic country determined to move forward rather than look back.

Above: Monks walking in the shade of trees on the road from Angkor Thom.

Left: Once lost to time and hidden in a dense forest, Angkor is now one of Southeast Asia's most visited attractions.

Phnom Penh is a city revitalized. The skyline of Cambodia's once sleepy capital has been pierced by its first high-rise building and the red dirt roads, now sealed, are filled with gleaming SUVs and swarms of buzzing motorcycles.

For a city that has endured more than its share of bloodshed and destruction, today's youthful exuberance and palpable energy are welcomed by residents and visitors alike. Confirming that the country's future is indeed bright, the bourgeoning capital city is now home to exquisite Buddhist temples, chic boutiques and relaxed riverside dining and entertainment venues, all of which make a visit interesting and exciting.

Yet despite the positive change being witnessed today, any time spent in Phnom Penh must still include reflective visits to the sites of the country's horrific past. Two of the most visited places in Phnom Penh are still Camp Cheoung Ek, one of many infamous Killing Fields sites, and Tuol Sleng Genocide Museum, a former high school that became a torture centre known as S-21.

Above left: Phnom Penh is rapidly evolving into one of Southeast Asia's most vibrant and energetic cities.

Above: The mysterious stone carvings of Angkor captivate all who see them.

Opposite: Relatively undeveloped, it is still possible to discover deserted beaches.

Beyond the capital there is also much to explore. Without question the biggest draw for travellers is the UNESCO World Heritage Site of Angkor, an area so vast and inspiring that it requires several days to explore. Aside from the temples of Angkor there is the nearby town of Siem Reap to discover, Tonle Sap Lake and its floating villages, museums, bird sanctuaries, thriving markets and an emerging arts scene. Further west of Siem Reap, the historic town of Battambang has some of the finest examples of colonial-era architecture in the country and is also surrounded by verdant countryside and peaceful villages where life still moves at the speed of an ox-drawn cart.

Cambodia's 450-km (280-mile) coastline is once again attracting visitors who are discovering near deserted beaches and islands lapped by crystal-clear waters. Located just a few hours' drive from the capital, the resort towns of Sihanoukville, Kampot and Kep, once popular haunts of the former French colonials, now lure Phnom Penh's middle class to golden beaches.

For the visitor, Cambodia is a land of contrasts inhabited by resilient, forward-looking people whose art and culture continues to inspire. For these reasons and more, a personal journey to enchanting Cambodia is truly one of discovery.

Above: In Cambodia, the rules of the road are relaxed to say the least.

Geography and Climate

Bordered by Laos, Thailand and Vietnam, tropical Cambodia covers 180,040 km² (69,514 sq. miles), just half the size of neighbouring Vietnam. Divided into 20 provinces, Cambodia has a fertile central plain, the rice basket of the country, that is bound by two mountain ranges. The mighty Mekong River enters Cambodia from Laos and spills into the enormous Tonle Sap Lake, the source of the largely agrarian population's supply of freshwater fish.

The Cardamom Mountains in the southwest of the country include Phnom Aural, Cambodia's highest mountain at 1,770 m (5,807 ft). An extension of the Cardamoms, the Elephant Range runs south and southeast, at points rising to elevations of up to 1,000 m (3,280 ft).

Around two-thirds of the country has forest cover but in recent years much of this has become degraded by continued legal and illegal logging. Cambodia's remaining virgin forest is at risk but there are some safe havens and ecotourism is slowly gaining ground in the country. With its many endangered birds and fragile habitats, Cambodia

attracts birdwatchers particularly to the Tmatboey Thoeun Krasaing Ibis Tourism Site outside Siem Reap. The site was established by the Wildlife Conservation Society (WCS) to protect an endangered bird, the ibis. The ecotourism project protects the only known site where both Giant and White-shouldered Ibis breed and can be regularly sighted. The birds are found in the forest and villagers nearby have established hides from which they can be seen and work as guides to take visiting birdwatchers to them.

Cambodia also has an extensive coastline with beautiful beaches and islands. Few, however, have been developed and still wait for the country's tourism numbers to increase and the industry to mature.

Cambodia's climate is tropical and monsoonal with cool, wet and dry seasons of a similar length. The temperature and humidity are generally high and constant throughout the year with only small variations from an average of around 25°C (77°F). The cool season runs from November to February and, although daytime temperatures can still reach 30°C (86°F), evenings can be pleasantly cool. The hot season from March to May can top 40°C (104°F) but the rainy season that follows from June to October is more bearable as sporadic storms clear the air.

Left: Cambodia's wetlands are the habitat of several endangered species.

Above: Sunset in the sleepy riverside town of Kampot.

Left: Planting rice is a family affair. Everyone helps out to ease the burden of the backbreaking work.

A Brief History of Cambodia

Cambodia's history is a story of a rise to greatness and regional dominance, followed by gradual decline and one of mankind's most notoriously dark and brutal periods.

The earliest recorded evidence of human habitation in Cambodia was discovered in the northwest at the caves of Laang Spean. Here, pottery believed to date from the sixth millennium B.C. was unearthed. Archaeologists working in eastern Kompong Cham also discovered Neolithic and Bronze Age artefacts such as polished stone tools and pottery dating from between 3,000–500 B.C. Neolithic adzes have also been found in the Angkor region and Battambang Province.

Early Khmer settlements existed in what is today southern Vietnam as long ago as the first century. The coastal towns are known to have been important trading posts for merchants from India and China. In the sixth century, most Khmers were settled along the Tonle Sap and Mekong where they cultivated rice and caught the rivers' bountiful supplies of freshwater fish. The loose amalgamation of separate states, the most important of which was known as Funan, would later became unified as the Khmer Empire with the magnificent city and temples of Angkor at its heart.

These pages: Once the seat of Southeast Asia's greatest empire, Angkor fell into decline during the 15th century. For years it was lost to an encroaching forest until in 1907 a team of French archaeologists began restoration work that continues today. Angkor encompasses over 1,000 sites, the greatest of which is Angkor Wat, a magnificent temple constructed in the 12th century for King Suryavarman II.

The Khmer Empire

In the eighth century, Jayavarman II became the country's first monarch. Under his reign, an advanced irrigation system was implemented in Angkor that enabled the Khmer Empire to flourish. Jayavarman II is also credited with building the first of the great Angkorian temples. During the 10th and 11th centuries, many of Angkor's important alliances fractured and a succession of kings were involved in conflicts and power struggles. Under the reign of Suryavarman II wars were fought with Champa or what is today central Vietnam. It was also Suryavarman II who ordered Angkor Wat to be constructed as a devotional act for the Hindu god, Vishnu. In 1177, Champa reaped revenge for its earlier defeat by sailing up the Mekong and into the Tonle Sap, sacking Angkor and executing King Dharanindravarman II. A year later, however, Champa was beaten by the Khmer army and Jayavarman VII was crowned.

In the years that followed some of Angkor's greatest temples were built including Angkor Thom, at the heart of which sits the spectacular Bayon, and Preah Khan, Ta Prohm and several more.

From the eighth to the 13th centuries, the Khmer Empire ruled over a vast region encompassing what today are Cambodia, northeast Thailand, southern Laos and southern Vietnam. However, five centuries of dominance were waning and in 1431 Angkor felt the full force of neighbouring Thailand's power when they attacked and captured the region, then moved the capital to Phnom Penh. Thailand's force was still being felt in 1794 when they held the provinces of Siem Reap and Battambang.

Above: Murals on walls within the compound of the Silver Pagoda date from 1903.

Top: Wat Thommanon is one of Angkor's smaller but no less beautiful temples.

The French Colonial Era

Left: Many of the French colonial-era buildings in Phnom Penh have fallen into disrepair and are desperately in need of renovation.

Below: Fortunately some, like this building in Kampot, have been restored.

In the early to mid-1800s, much of Cambodia was a vassal state of Thailand, with the east of the country being controlled by Vietnam. When the French arrived in the region they viewed Cambodia's weakened state as an opportunity to expand their power in Indochina. In 1863 King Norodom's hand was forced into signing a treaty of protection with the French. A year later Cambodia was annexed and became a French colony. Despite an initial rebellion by the Khmers, 75 years of French rule followed. For Cambodia's impotent monarchy, however, colonization was seen as necessary for the survival of the royal court. The French also regained control of Battambang and Siem Reap – which translates as Thais defeated – from Thailand.

Following World War II there was growing resistance to French rule and the Khmer Issarak or "Free Khmer" movement was formed to fight for independence. In 1953, King Norodom Sihanouk threw his weight behind Cambodia's bid for freedom by dissolving parliament and declaring martial law. On 9 November 1953, Cambodia declared independence, an action that was internationally recognized in May of 1954.

The Rise of the Khmer Rouge

In 1970, Prince Sihanouk was toppled by a U.S.-backed coup, a move that further destabilized the country. In 1973, the U.S. began an eight-month bombing campaign dropping hundreds of thousands of tons of bombs across Cambodia. Many rural Cambodians sought refuge in Phnom Penh, one of the few places that was not being bombed, and the population grew to over two million. In 1975, two weeks before the fall of South Vietnam, the Khmer Rouge regime came to power under Solath Sar, or Pol Pot as he was also known. The years that followed were the most bloody and brutal in Cambodian history.

Under the leadership of Pol Pot and his henchmen, Cambodians were marched out of Phnom Penh and forced to work in collective farms. Educated citizens were massacred and the calendar was started at Year Zero. Estimates vary, but over 1.7 million people are thought to have been massacred under the regime and many more died of hunger and disease.

In 1978, Vietnamese troops overthrew the Khmer Rouge but when they withdrew from the country civil war broke out and several groups, including the Khmer Rouge tried to gain power. The United Nations worked for a peace settlement that resulted in elections in 1993 and Norodom Sihanouk was once again crowned. The Khmer Rouge leader, Pol Pot, escaped justice and died aged 73 in 1998. Shortly before he died he was held prisoner by former Khmer Rouge members who had accused him of betraying the movement he had once led.

In 2001, Cambodia's King Sihanouk signed legislation for a special tribunal to prosecute members of the Khmer Rouge. A series of delays and squabbles over the financing of the UN-backed trial prevented the judicial process from moving forward. Many saw the delays as a ruse to derail the trials. Those that have faced the courts have received light sentences.

A Brave New Future

For the past two decades Cambodian politics have been dominated by Prime Minister Samdech Hun Sen, a former soldier in the Khmer Rouge. Despite considerable challenges and a widening division between rich and poor, Cambodia is enjoying a period of peace and relative stability. It is also experiencing huge investment from countries such as China and Korea. With increased development, a youthful population and increased tourism, Cambodia and its resilient population are now bravely looking towards a new and brighter future.

Left: Mines on display at the Landmine Museum on the outskirts of Siem Reap are a permanent reminder of Cambodia's deadly legacy.

Opposite: Monks walk past the Independence Monument in Phnom Penh. Built in 1958, it is a memorial to Cambodia's war dead and to independence from the French five years earlier.

The People

Cambodia's population of just over 14 million is predominantly ethnic Khmer and almost all are Buddhist. Chinese immigrants make up about four per cent of the population. As in neighbouring Thailand, the Chinese have assimilated into Cambodian culture and, as Cambodia becomes more prosperous, are beginning to dominate the business and financial sector. The Vietnamese account for one per cent. They are involved in much of the country's fishing industry, with many fisheries at the floating villages on Tonle Sap Lake.

Above: A market trader wearing the traditional 'krama', a check headscarf used for protection from the sun.

Right: Despite a huge increase in the number of cars and motorcycles, for the poor a bicycle is still the only option.

Below: The vast Tonle Sap is home to many floating villages where locals make their living almost exclusively from fishing.

Right: A young monk caught in the half light at Angkor Wat.

Cambodia also has a significant population of Cham or Khmer Muslims who adopted their faith from Malays who settled in Kampot in the 17th century. Descendants of the former kingdom of Champa, they were heavily persecuted by the Khmer Rouge. Today the majority of Cham Muslims live beside the Mekong River and Tonle Sap.

A handful of minority ethnic groups are scattered throughout the hills of the northeastern borders with Vietnam and Laos. These include the Kui in Preah Vihear Province, the Pnong in Mondulkiri, Ratanakiri, Kratie and Stung Treng Provinces and the Krung also in Ratanakiri and Stung Treng Provinces.

Religion

Buddhism arrived in Cambodia during the 13th century and soon became the official religion of the country. Today, around 90 per cent of the population follows Theravada Buddhism, although elements of animism and ancestor worship have also been integrated into many Buddhist rituals and festivals.

Traditionally the village temple played a central role within Cambodian society, ensuring cohesion of the community and providing a basic education for the poor. During the Khmer Rouge years of 1975 to 1979, however, many monks were forced to do manual labour or were murdered and the majority of Cambodia's temples were destroyed.

During the 1980s, as part of a concerted effort to rebuild Cambodian society, religion began to play a key role in society once again, temples were rebuilt and Buddhism is now recognized in the Cambodian Constitution as the state religion. The Cambodian *sangha* or assembly is divided into two distinct sects: the Mahanikaya sect, 90 per cent of which is made up of monks, and the smaller Thammayut sect that was introduced by the Thais in the mid-nineteenth century and became popular with royalists and the ruling class.

Left: Many temples were destroyed during the Khmer Rouge era but have been restored. Today, Cambodians are once again free to worship. Buddhism is the state religion and monks play an important role in the spiritual wellbeing of the people and education of the young.

Opposite right: Temples feature ornately carved details painted in red and gold.

Opposite left: Spirit houses are a common sight due to the Cambodian belief that when a piece of land is disturbed the spirits that inhabit it need to be appeased. Daily offerings of flowers, food and incense are made by the faithful at the spirit house.

Theravada Buddhism is a tolerant religion based on three concepts: dharma, the doctrine of the Buddha; karma, the belief that your life and future incarnations depend on your deeds and misdeeds; and sangha, the religious community where man can improve his karma. Nirvana, it is said, can be reached by earning merit. A Buddhist's pilgrimage through existence is a constant attempt to distance himself or herself from the world and finally to achieve complete detachment, or nirvana. Every young Buddhist man is expected to enter the monkhood for a short period of his life, an act which earns great merit for the family. The daily ritual of offering food to monks, worship and donations are all considered merit-making actions that will contribute to a better life after rebirth.

The Cham communities in the south-east practise Islam. Although many mosques were destroyed during the Khmer Rouge rule, today there are estimated to be around 250 in the country, many of which are in Kompong Cham Province.

There is a small Christian community in Cambodia, mainly among the Chinese populations in Phnom Penh, while animism is practised by the country's hill tribes.

Above: A woman offers a jasmine garland to an image of Buddha at a shrine in Siem Reap.

Left: Lotus flowers and money are often placed in the hands of Buddha images at temples.

Above: In the early morning, lines of monks can be seen collecting alms. They wait in silence outside shops and homes for offerings of food.

Left: Buddha images at a shrine within the complex of the Silver Pagoda, Phnom Penh.

Cambodian Cuisine

With the growing interest in Cambodia as a destination, the country's cuisine is currently undergoing somewhat of a renaissance. Many of the delicious traditional dishes are being revived and refined for the tables of an ever-increasing number of restaurants.

Rice, which is grown on the central plains, is fundamental to the Cambodian diet as well as a wide variety of freshwater fish from the Mekong River and the Tonle Sap. Cambodia also produces fermented fish paste known as *prahoc* and fish sauce, both of which are used to add flavour and saltiness to dishes.

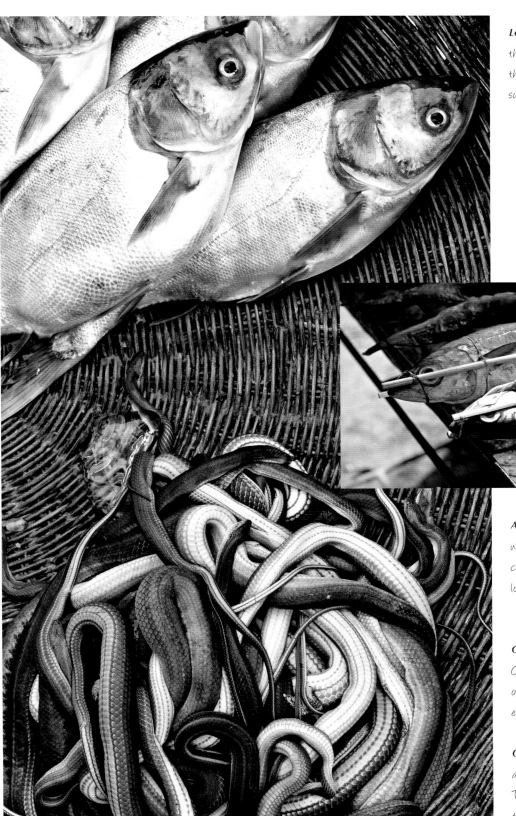

Left: Fresh catches of fish from the Tonle Sap are sold daily in the morning markets. Wild food such as snake is also popular.

Above: Mackerel caught in the waters off the country's extensive coastline being barbecued in a local market.

Opposite above: A staple of the Cambodian diet, steamed rice or sticky rice is eaten at almost every meal.

Opposite below: Although not as spicy as food in neighbouring Thailand, chillies are still central to Cambodian cuisine.

Cambodian cooks draw on a number of influences to create their distinctive cuisine, namely the foods of neighbouring Laos, Thailand and Vietnam. Flavoursome yet without the searing chilli heat of Thai food, many Western visitors find the food a pleasant surprise. The classic Khmer dish is *amok*, a mix of fish, coconut milk, lemongrass, herbs and spices baked in a banana leaf. Fragrant and delicious, *amok* can be considered the country's national dish.

When dining Cambodian-style, typically, soup is ordered with almost every meal. Local favourites include *somlar machu banle*, a sour fish soup, and *somlar chapek*, pork soup with ginger, a commonly used ingredient. A fish or meat dish and vegetables will also be served to accompany the staple of rice.

Outside influences also include Chinese noodle dishes and, a culinary legacy of the French colonial era, the baguette, which Cambodians enjoy warmed over charcoal, split and filled with pâté, pork, raw papaya and chilli sauce.

Visitors are also likely to see a wide variety of less familiar snacks being sold by street vendors. These include fried crickets, tarantulas, termites, bee larvae and freshwater snails. Some barbecue restaurants also serve crocodile and python meat.

The restaurant scene in Phnom Penh and Siem Reap is blossoming. For those who want to continue to enjoy a taste of Cambodia when they return home, there are also several inspiring cookery schools running one-day courses. An enjoyable way to gain valuable insight into the food and culture, the courses are typically hands-on and the classes are small. Aspiring chefs learn to cook three or four dishes, dine together at the end of the day and receive recipes to take home.

These pages: Most Cambodians buy freshly cooked food from street-side vendors and in the bustling morning and evening markets. Noodle soups are popular and are eaten for breakfast, lunch or dinner.

Arts and Crafts

During the Khmer Rouge years, the brutal regime made a concerted effort to wipe out artists and craftsmen, and they very nearly succeeded. Many of the traditional arts, particularly Cambodian dance, were almost lost forever. Fortunately, young people are now being retrained and Cambodian craftsmen and women are once again being acknowledged for their skills and unique aesthetic.

Breathing Life into Dying Arts

Left: At Artisans d'Angkor, stone carving is one of many disciplines being taught in an attempt to save craft knowledge.

Below: Cambodia is being re-established as a producer of high quality silk. The silk worms are bred in rural farms before the cocoons are processed, spun, then woven into lengths of exquisite silk.

One organization that has worked tirelessly to promote the rich heritage and evolution of Cambodian crafts is Artisans d'Angkor. Established in 1997 and originally under EU funding, the business is now self-financing. Each year it trains artisans in traditional crafts such as lacquerware, weaving, silverware and stone carving. After completing their training, many of the artists go on to set up their own workshops. Although most of the work produced is a reproduction of Angkor-era arts or deeply influenced by the period, with exposure to the international marketplace and

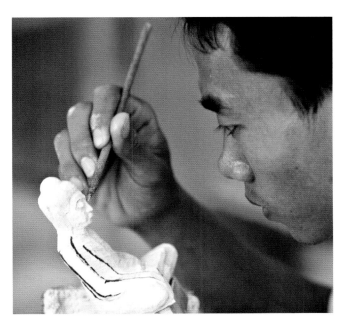

the demands of visitors, many artists are now developing an individual style.

In Siam Reap Artisans d'Angkor have a shop in the town centre and a workshop where visitors can see the crafts being made. Further out of town there is a silk weaving centre and another shop close to Angkor Wat. Yet Cambodian art and craft is not all about maintaining traditions. In Phnom Penh there is also a vibrant emerging modern arts scene fuelled by graduates who have returned from studying abroad.

Left: Carving small Buddha images from soapstone is painstaking work.

Below: A painter at Artisans d'Angkor works on a reproduction of an ancient Khmer mural.

Apsara Dance

It is thought that 90 per cent of Cambodia's dancers and musicians were killed during the Khmer Rouge years. The chain of oral traditions passed down from generation to generation by masters of the arts was almost broken. Organizations such as Cambodian Living Arts tracked down a few survivors and employed them to train a new generation of musicians and dancers.

Cambodian classical dance drama is based on the epic poem, *Ramayana*, which has its origins in Indian literature. The dance also draws on the traditions of Indian court dance and is often referred to as Apsara after the female nymphs described in Hindu mythology that were born as dancers to the gods. Images of celestial Apsara dancers dating from the 12th century and earlier can be seen carved on the temple walls at Angkor, evidence that this highly stylized art form has been part of Cambodian culture for centuries.

A Cambodian dance troupe, dressed in glittering costumes, elaborate headwear and masks, performs with beauty and grace, their slow movements punctuated by a percussive ensemble that sits to the side of the stage. Acts of the drama are often separated by a narrative read out by one of the musicians.

Cambodia's growing tourism industry has contributed to the revival of traditional dance. In Phnom Penh, regular performances by troupes such as the Children of Bassac can be seen. In Siem Reap, five star hotels such as the Raffles Grand Hotel d'Angkor host regular performances of beautifully choreographed Apsara dance drama accompanied by live music. Guests enjoy an intimate setting in the gardens of one of Cambodia's grandest hotels, a mesmerizing and graceful performance, followed by a gourmet barbecue.

Below: Images of 'Apsara' dancers feature in many of the temple carvings at Angkor.

Right: Once almost totally wiped out by the Khmer Rouge, today the beautiful art of Khmer dance can be seen at dinner shows staged in hotels in Siem Reap and Phnom Penh.

Above: Dancers perform graceful, stylized movements and hand gestures to the accompaniment of traditional music.

Chapter 2: Phnom Penh

Situated at the confluence of three rivers, the Mekong, the Tonle Sap and the Bassac, Phnom Penh bristles with the energy of a youthful population of over 2 million. With investment pouring in from China, the dusty red dirt roads are long gone and a new modern skyline is quickly emerging.

Although the pace of change in the city is remarkable, architectural gems from the French colonial era can still be found in a network of side streets, along with the Central Market, a stunning art deco building and now home to Phnom Penh's gold traders. Highlights include the beautifully restored Royal Palace and Silver Pagoda, and the National Museum with its inspiring collection of Khmer art and sculpture.

This page: In the last few years, Phnom Penh has experienced a boom in construction and an explosion of traffic on the roads. However, more traditional and sedate methods of transport still remain (above). Guaranteed to assault the senses, local markets are chaotic and colourful places to explore (right).

Left: Some of the former French mansions have been restored and are used by international organizations such as UNESCO.

Above: The Foreign Correspondents Club or FCC in Phnom Penh is a popular bar, restaurant and hotel overlooking the Mekong River. The former French colonial-era villa is open to non-members.

The Royal Palace

Left: The Royal Palace complex dates from 1866. It houses Buddha statues and religious and royal artefacts including an emerald Buddha encrusted with jewels. The Throne Hall, shown left, was the second to be built on the site and is topped by a 60-m (197-ft) spire. Inside, the ceiling is decorated with beautiful murals of scenes from the 'Reamker'.

Above: Hor Samran Phirun pavilion within the palace grounds was built in 1917 to house musical instruments and regalia for royal processions. Several other ornate pavilions in the grounds include an original constructed as an open-air venue for classical Khmer dance.

The Silver Pagoda

This page: The Silver Pagoda, part of the Royal Palace compound in Phnom Penh, has a floor covered with 5,000 silver tiles. Among the many treasures housed here is a solid gold Buddha weighing 90 kg (198 lb) and encrusted with 9,584 diamonds. It is also known as Wat Preah Keo Morokat or the Temple of the Emerald Buddha and was traditionally the place where royal ceremonies were held. Several stupas here contain the ashes of former kings and queens of Cambodia.

Above: *A detail from a stupa at the Silver Pagoda.*

Left: *One of several stupas in the grounds of the Silver Pagoda, this one contains the ashes of King Suramarit and Queen Kossomak, the father and mother of former King Sihanouk.*

Tuol Sleng Genocide Museum

Left: A visit to Tuol Sleng Genocide Museum, along with the Killing Fields, is a harrowing but necessary part of a trip to Phnom Penh. Located in a suburb of the city, the former school was known to the Khmer Rouge as S-21 and was used as a centre for torture.

Camp Cheoung Ek Killing Fields

Below and right: Camp Cheoung Ek lies 15 km (nine miles) southwest of the city and was the burial site for those tortured and killed in S-21. In 1980, 129 mass graves were found here and 8,985 corpses unearthed. Today, a large stupa contains the bones and remnants of clothing as a memorial to the victims.

The National Museum

This page: The distinctive ochre-red building of the National Museum in the heart of Phnom Penh houses a wonderful collection of over 5,000 Khmer works of art and sculptures. Streets around the museum are renowned for the boutiques and shops selling arts and crafts.

Wat Phnom

Below: Wat Phnom features a large seated bronze Buddha and other images and painted walls that depict his earlier reincarnations, along with scenes from the 'Reamker'. The temple is extremely popular with local worshippers.

Above: Wat Phnom is the hilltop temple from which Phnom Penh takes its name. Thought to date from 1372, the temple is accessed by a stairway guarded by carved lions and serpents or 'nagas'. The stupa contains the ashes of King Ponhea Yat who is credited with moving the capital from Angkor to Phnom Penh in 1434 after it was sacked by the Siamese.

The Central Market

This page: The fabulous Psar Thmei, more commonly known as the Central Market, is a striking art deco building dating back to 1935. Here you can buy just about anything including shoes, clothing and souvenirs. The market, which has recently benefited from restoration work, can be accessed by four main entrances that lead into the central dome. Once a fresh produce market, the area within the main dome now houses gold and jewellery traders.

Chapter 3: Siem Reap

As the gateway to Angkor, Siem Reap is Cambodia's most visited town. Located just eight km (five miles) from the ancient temple sites, the town has benefited from the massive influx of tourists and the establishment of many new luxury hotels and resorts.

Although everyone who stays in Siem Reap is there for daily visits to Angkor, the town and surrounding area should not be overlooked. A visit to the Angkor National Museum explains the history of Angkor in a clear and concise manner and is an excellent and informative precursor to a trip to the ruins. It also includes a stunning collection of over 1,000 Buddha images. Golfers also come from all over Asia to play at the Phokeethra Country Club.

Above: Angkor National Museum is an excellent facility purpose built to house the many treasures of Angkor.

Below: Colourful Siem Reap has much to offer including excellent restaurants, bars and boutiques.

Right: Regarded as one of the finest hotels in Southeast Asia, the Raffles Grand Hotel d'Angkor in Siem Reap invites guests to experience the ambience of a bygone era, outstanding service and modern day conveniences.

Above and right: Siem Reap now has several golf courses including the Phokeethra Country Club located just 20 km (12 miles) from the town centre. Golfers come to enjoy the beautiful tropical course with sweeping fairways and attractive green fees.

Left: In the morning, Siem Reap's central market comes alive with traders selling fresh vegetables and fish from the Tonle Sap.

Above: The Foreign Correspondents Club, a former French governor's mansion, also includes a new block to the rear that serves as a boutique hotel.

The centre of Siem Reap features a pleasant market, boutiques selling local crafts and several cafés. A taste of local life can also be found at Phsar Leu, the town's central market on the outskirts of town, and at the nearby floating villages on Tonle Sap. In the evenings, a good place to relax is at the Foreign Correspondents Club or with pre-dinner cocktails at the distinctly colonial Elephant Bar in the refined Raffles Grand Hotel d'Angkor. A host of bars and restaurants on Pub Street also draw the crowds, including the popular Red Piano Bar, where Angelina Jolie is said to have taken a break from filming, an act that has been immortalized by the bar's 'Tomb Raider' cocktail.

Left: Once a sleepy backwater, today Siem Reap welcomes hundreds of thousands of visitors a year. Many of the old shophouses have been converted into chic boutiques, cafés, bars and restaurants. There is also a popular night market for souvenir shopping.

Chong Kneas Floating Village

This page: The floating village of Chong Kneas provides visitors with a fascinating break from the temples of Angkor. Located a 20 minute tuk-tuk ride from the centre of the town, this village is a ramshackle collection of stilted houses and floating homes that move with the seasonal rise and fall of the Tonle Sap.

The Vietnamese at Chong Kneas Floating Village, make their living from catching and farming fish, and from selling essential items from floating shops. There are also some crocodile farms at the village. Although Chong Kneas is the most visited and the easiest to get to, there are many other floating villages along the shores of the Tonle Sap.

This page: There are two communities at Chong Kneas. The Cambodians tend to inhabit the stilted houses, while the Vietnamese are totally waterborne.

Chapter 4: Temples of Angkor

The truly magnificent UNESCO World Heritage Site of Angkor encompasses more than 30 temples and ancient buildings spread over a vast area. Angkor Wat itself covers an area of one square kilometre (247 acres) and comprises three levels and a central tower. The entranceway is particularly impressive. Inside the confines of the temple, the inner and outer walls are covered with exquisite bas-reliefs.

Angkor Wat

The Angkor period began in 802 AD when Jayavarman II established the cult of Devaraja or God King and declared himself a universal monarch. Following his death in 850 AD, Angkor was ruled by a succession of 38 kings until the end of the Angkor period in 1432 AD when the capital was relocated to Phnom Penh. High points of the empire were during the reign of King Suryavarman II from 1113–1150, a period that saw the construction of the magnificent Angkor Wat. From 1181–1220, under the instruction of King Jayavarman VII, Angkor's infrastructure was greatly expanded and many monuments built including Angkor Thom, the Bayon and Preah Khan. Angkor suffered gradual decline during the 14th century. The eventual relocation of the capital has been attributed to several factors: increasing attacks by the neighbouring Thais, pressure on natural resources from the large population and drought.

Left: There are several Buddha images within the confines of the ancient temple that are still cared for by monks from a nearby temple and presented with daily offerings.

Above: Regarded as the jewel in Angkor's crown, Angkor Wat is one of the wonders of Asia and a beautiful sight, night or day. At daybreak, the temple grounds are crowded with visitors waiting to watch the sunrise over the distinctive towers.

Right: The Apsara, a female nymph from Hindu mythology, is one of the most common images carved on the walls of Angkor Wat and other temples at the expansive site.

Above: Worn away by time and the elements, this Apsara at Angkor Wat is an almost ghostly image.

Above: The extensive galleries at Angkor Wat feature a wealth of exquisite bas-reliefs depicting Khmer legends and scenes from the 'Reamker'.

Opposite: It is impossible not to be impressed by the sheer scale and beauty of the temple. It is advisable to return to Angkor Wat at different times of the day to experience the changing quality of light. The galleries are particularly atmospheric.

Angkor Thom

Angkor Thom dates from the 12th and 13th centuries and was the last capital of the Khmer Empire. Enclosed by a moat and a three-km (one and three quarter-mile) wall, the area is entered through an impressive gateway.

Above and right: Today, Angkor Thom is one of Asia's most enchanting sights but at the height of the Khmer Empire must have been truly breathtaking. The Chinese diplomat who gazed upon its splendour in 1296 described it as a 'truly astonishing spectacle' with golden towers, bridges and Buddha images.

Bayon

At the heart of the Angkor Thom complex is the Bayon with 54 towers, most of which feature four massive carved faces.

Above: Located at the centre of Angkor Thom, the Bayon is undoubtedly one of the Angkor's most visually impressive and moving temples.

These pages: Built 100 years after Angkor Wat, the many towers of the Bayon feature over 200 carved faces. It is believed that the four faces on each tower are that of King Jayarvarman VII.

This page: Today, Apsaras still dance at Angkor even if it is for tourists instead of royalty. Here, a pair of dancers add a flash of vibrant colour amongst the grey lichen-covered walls of the Bayon.

Ta Prohm

Ta Prohm is a sprawling temple complex and the site of some of Angkor's most memorable imagery. The main temple was lost to jungle for centuries. When the site was reclaimed, the massive trees that straddled the walls were left in place. It is a fascinating temple to explore and great for photography. Bayon and Ta Prohm were used as sets in the film *Tomb Raider*.

Above and right: Constructed from the mid-12th century to the early 13th century, Ta Prohm is one of the largest sites in Angkor. Inscriptions found at the site but now removed to a museum stated that Ta Prohm controlled 3,140 villages in the area.

This page: When archaeologists discovered Ta Prohm in the mid-19th century they only cleared trees and undergrowth from the main pathways. Today, it remains one of the most atmospheric of the many Angkor sites.

Opposite: The entire complex is enclosed by a wall and within there are many passageways and galleries, some housing Buddha images. Ta Prohm also has some fine examples of carved Apsaras.

Above and right: The outer walls feature some wonderful carvings which turn green with lichen and moss during the rainy season.

Phreah Khan

This page: Phreah Khan, meaning 'sacred sword' dates from around 1191 and was built during the reign of King Jayavarman VII. Although it is a Buddhist temple, it also features shrines honouring Hindu deities. Similar to Ta Prohm, Phreah Khan has been encroached upon by the forest. This, combined with its covered galleries and passageways, make it a very atmospheric temple to explore.

Above: The main sanctuary at Phreah Khan features four covered passageways, although many sections of the roof have now collapsed, leading to the central stupa.

Left: One of the joys of exploring the temples of Angkor is discovering exquisite carvings among the ruins.

Above left: Phreah Khan encompasses over 57 hectares (140 acres) and is accessed by a long paved causeway lined with carved figures of gods and demons.

Banteay Srei

There are several fine temples beyond Angkor, one of the best being Banteay Srei. It is worth taking the 38 km (24-mile) ride out here, if only to enjoy a drive through the beautiful countryside. The temple is constructed of sandstone that has a pinkish tinge and its delicate bas-reliefs are in excellent condition. Due to looting, the sculptures at the site are replicas. The remaining originals can be seen at the National Museum in Phnom Penh.

These pages: Banteay Srei, or the Citadel of Women, is a Hindu temple dedicated to Shiva. The temple has been dated to 967 and was rediscovered by the French in 1914. It features some of the most intricate and impressive carving to be found at Angkor. The pink sandstone temple is particularly beautiful in the early morning or evening light.

This page: The sandstone carvings at Banteay Srei are in excellent condition and in some sections are totally covered with delicately crafted leaves and flowers. It is easy to understand why when French archaeologists came across the pink temple they called it the 'jewel of Khmer art'.

Right: The inner sanctuary of Banteay Srei is off-limits to visitors in order to help preserve the stunning craftsmanship. The corners of the central tower are protected by stone guardians and the outer walls are carved with scenes from the Ramayana including a battle between the monkeys, Sugreeva and Vali, and the capture of Sita, the wife of Rama.

Below: A section of the southern library features a stunningly beautiful carving that depicts Ravana shaking Mount Kailash, the home of Lord Shiva, the destroyer of evil and sorrow. The story tells that Shiva then pinned down Ravana until he cried out for mercy. After his release, he became a devotee of Shiva.

Battambang

The town of Battambang is 175 km (109 miles) west of Siem Reap. It is possible to hire a taxi and visit the town as a day excursion but an overnight stay is recommended. Visitors can enjoy a pleasant day wandering the streets of the old town, exploring temples and markets, and dining in open-fronted restaurants.

Below: Once an important administrative town for the French, Battambang has its own unique charm. Although some areas are rundown and neglected, many of the old buildings are now benefiting from restoration.

Left: For many visitors, the sight of lines of monks collecting alms in the early morning is the most enchanting and exotic experience. Monks take the donations of food back to the temple. They are not allowed to eat after noon until daybreak.

Left and below right:
Battambang has many of Cambodia's best preserved colonial-era buildings dating from the early 1900s and several beautiful old temples. The busy commercial town is also the second largest in Cambodia and sits at the heart of an area renowned as the 'rice bowl' of the country.

Left: This classic French period building on Battambang's riverfront and now owned by the Bank of Cambodia has been lovingly restored to its former glory.

Chapter 5: South Coast

Cambodia is blessed with an extensive coastline of beautiful and mostly deserted beaches and islands. Popular getaways during the French colonial era, they exude an ambience of faded charm and life that moves at an unhurried pace. Still very much free of the commercialism and over development found in neighbouring Thailand, Cambodia's sleepy resort towns are once again finding favour with lovers of sun, sea and sand.

Sihanoukville

Sihanoukville is a port and resort town 160 km (100 miles) southwest of Phnom Penh. Visitors can enjoy empty beaches, fresh seafood, clear blue sea and nearby islands.

Right: Cambodia's southern coastline is lapped by crystal-clear waters. Boats wait at the jetty to take visitors out to near deserted islands.

Opposite: Ochheuteal Beach in Sihanoukville is becoming increasingly popular with overseas visitors. The three-kilometre (nearly two-mile) stretch of sand is lined with bars and restaurants serving freshly grilled seafood. Fishing boats offer trips to nearby islands.

Above: Ochheuteal Beach is the perfect place to relax and enjoy an ice-cold beer as the sun sets.

Left: A hawker at Ochheuteal Beach offers freshly cooked langoustine. Fishing boats along the coastline head out to sea in the early evening, returning at daybreak with their catch.

Right: Constructed in 1966, the monument of the two golden lions in Sihanoukville is the town's most distinctive landmark. It acts as a roundabout on the road to Ochheuteal Beach.

Opposite: The monument at Independence Square on Ekareach Street in Sihanoukville marks the country's liberation from colonial rule and honours its war dead.

Kampot

While the nearby resort town of Sihanoukville has long since woken up to tourism, Kampot still slumbers. With its quiet streets, riverfront cafés and bars and French colonial architecture, this enchanting town has a relaxed ambience and is easily explored on foot or by bicycle.

This page: Kampot is beginning to benefit from Sihanoukville's increasing number of visitors. The town makes an excellent base for a few day's relaxation and exploring Bokor National Park, waterfalls and farms growing the famous Kampot pepper. Tuk-tuks can be hired by the day or the hour and are a convenient and trouble-free way to get to see all the sights.

Above: *A close-up of a stone figure on a temple wall. Kampot has several interesting old temples to discover, along with other sites of historical interest, such as the old French railway station.*

Above: *During the Khmer Rouge era, Kampot's old French-built bridge was partially destroyed. Now repaired it once again allows locals to cross Prek Kampong Bay.*

Left: *Monks can be seen walking barefoot to collect alms throughout the year with the exception of the rainy season when they stay in the temple.*

Kep

Kep is another delightfully laidback beach town with more faded French charm. Once a popular weekend destination for Phnom Penh's wealthy, the promenade is lined with abandoned villas that remind visitors of its former glory and future potential. A big attraction on the seafront is the Kep crab market. Each morning, Vietnamese girls gather on the promenade to sell their catch.

This page: From daybreak, girls haul their catch of fresh crabs onto Kep's promenade and crowds gather to barter for a good price. Every now and again, a basket will be returned to the water and a new one hauled ashore. Next to the crab market, a row of restaurants serves up a variety of seafood and, of course, crab.

Above: Kep's extensive and well-built promenade is evidence of its former glory. Many of the abandoned villas in the area are being rebuilt in anticipation of a tourism boom in coming years.

Right: Kep is known for having the best crab in Cambodia but locals will tell you that the catch is a fraction of what it used to be and the crabs are much smaller.

Getting About

The majority of travellers to Cambodia arrive at one of two airports: Phnom Penh International Airport, located 13 km (eight miles) from the city centre, or the new Siem Reap International Airport seven km (just over four miles) from the town centre. Both airports are served by regular flights from Thailand, Laos, Vietnam, Singapore and Malaysia.

Above: The 'romauk' or 'tuk-tuk', a motorcycle that pulls a carriage, is one of Cambodia's most popular forms of transport.

Visitors from most countries can apply for a visa on arrival for a fee of US$20. The visa is valid for one month. No vaccinations are required to enter Cambodia but typhoid, hepatitis A and B, rabies and tetanus are recommended. Fixed-fare taxi rides from the airports to hotels are available for around US$7.

In common with all developing countries, travel in Cambodia can be a challenge if you wish to explore rural areas. Generally though, the network of roads connecting major towns is in very good condition. The country is also served by several domestic airports but flights can often be cancelled if there are not enough passengers.

Left: Sales of motorcycles in Phnom Penh have boomed recently and it is the vehicle of choice for many. They can be hired cheaply but beware, the rules of the road are non-existent.

Bus travel in Cambodia is inexpensive and a good option if you choose a reputable company and a VIP coach. Advanced booking of your seat is recommended. For long journeys, many people opt to hire an air-conditioned taxi at an agreed daily rate but if you do this ask around and bargain hard as prices can vary considerably. It is also advisable to agree your exact itinerary and expectations before embarking on a journey as some drivers will use any deviation from the agreed route as an excuse to ask for more money.

Within towns and cities there are several choices for getting around. These include the *cyclopousse*, a tricycle-rickshaw, the *motodup* or motorcycle taxi and the *romauk*, a motorcycle that pulls a carriage and that is now more commonly referred to as a *tuk-tuk*. Prices should always be agreed in advance and bargaining is expected. In Cambodia's tropical climate, *tuk-tuks* are an excellent way to get around and preferable to the confines of a car. You can hire a *tuk-tuk* and driver, many of whom speak good English, for between US$15–18 a day for running around Siem Reap and Angkor. For longer trips out to places such as Banteay Srei, expect the fee to rise to $25. Drivers usually wait near hotels and the concierge should be able to assist with negotiations. In Phnom Penh daily rates can be $20–25 a day.

Bicycles are available for hire at shops and hotels in all popular destinations and are a very good way to explore the towns and countryside, particularly Angkor. However, caution is advised. In recent years traffic in Cambodia has increased rapidly, the standard of driving is very poor and the hazards on the road are many.

Visitors to Cambodia can also travel by river which is an excellent way to gain a new perspective on the country. The most popular route is between Phnom Penh and Siem Reap. Journey times vary depending on the season. In the wet season when the rivers are high, the journey can be as little as 4 hours. During the dry season the service can often be cancelled. Passengers should also be aware that breakdowns are not uncommon and that safety measures do not meet any recognized standard.

One company operating luxury cruises on the Tonle Sap and down the Mekong River is Compagnie Fluviale du Mekong. Passengers can also travel between Siem Reap and Ho Chi Minh City in Vietnam. The safety and accommodation are designed to meet international standards. The cruise schedule is limited to the wet season months.

Around Angkor there are several interesting travel options including hot air ballooning and a fixed line balloon ride to view Angkor Wat from above, and helicopter rides.

Resources

Contacts

The following websites may provide useful information when organizing your trip to Cambodia.

Angkor: http://whc.unesco.org/en/list/668

Arts and crafts: www.artisansdangkor.com and
    www.cambodianlivingarts.org

Golf: The Phokeethra Country Club
    www.phokeethragolf.com

Hotels: Raffles Grand Hotel d'Angkor www.raffles.com
    and Sofitel Angkor Phokeethra Golf & Spa Resort
    www.sofitel.com

Monument Books: www.monument-books.com/bookshop

River cruises: www.cfmekong.com

Tourism information: www.tourismcambodia.com

Visa and travel advisory: www.canbypublications.com/
    cambodia/visas.htm

Airlines

Siem Reap: www.siemreapair.com
Thai Airways: www.thaiairways.com
Bangkok Airways: www.bangkokair.com
Vietnam Airlines: www.vietnamairlines.com
AirAsia: www.airasia.com

Bibliography and Recommended Reading

Zhou Dagvan, translated by Peter Harris. 2007. *A Record of Cambodia: The Land and Its People.* Silkworm Books.
Haing Ngor, H. *Surviving the Killing Fields.* Basic Books.
Dawn Rooney, D. *Angkor: Cambodia's Wondrous Khmer Temples.* Odyssey.
Shippen, M. 2005. *Traditional Ceramics of South East Asia.* A&C Black.

Acknowledgements

Many thanks to Didier Lamoot at the Sofitel Phnom Penh Phokeethra, Peter Lucas at Sofitel Angkor Phokeethra Golf & Spa Resort, Robert Hauck at the truly magnificent Raffles Grand Hotel d'Angkor, Siem Reap, David Bowden and not forgetting Madam Aong.

About the Author

Mick Shippen is a freelance writer and photographer. Based in Thailand since 1997, he currently lives in Laos. Mick travels extensively throughout Asia conducting research for articles and taking photographs for local and international newspapers and magazines. A keen biker, he spends his spare time motorcycling and has toured extensively on and off-road in Asia. He is the author of *The Traditional Ceramics of South East Asia*, as well as a contributing writer for the books *To Asia with Love, To Myanmar with Love* and *To Thailand with Love*. His images can been viewed at www.mickshippen.com

Index

This edition published in the United Kingdom in 2019 by John Beaufoy Publishing,
11 Blenheim Court, 316 Woodstock Road, Oxford OX2 7NS, England
www.johnbeaufoy.com

10 9 8 7 6 5 4 3 2 1

ISBN 978-1-912081-07-3

Original design by Glyn Bridgewater
Cover design by Ginny Zeal
Cartography by William Smuts
Project management by Rosemary Wilkinson

Printed and bound in Malaysia by Times Offset (M) Sdn. Bhd.

Cover captions and credits:
Back cover (left to right): *Siem Reap* © Mick Shippen; *Ta Prohm* © Mick Shippen; *Ochheuteal Beach in
Sihanoukville* © Mick Shippen; *A restored former French colonial mansion* © Mick Shippen. Front cover top (left to right):
Central Market, Phnom Penh © Mick Shippen; *Chillies and lime, common flavours of Cambodian cuisine* © Mick
Shippen; *Monks on their daily tour in Phnom Penh,* © Shutterstcock.com/swiss macky;
The monument of the two golden lions in Sihanoukville, © Mick Shippen.
Front cover (main image): Angkor Wat, © Shutterstock.com/Amnartk